A VETERAN'S HOME BUYING JOURNEY

FROM RANKS TO RICHES

HOW YOUR VA HOME LOAN HELPS YOU: AVOID THE RENTING TRAP, BUY A HOME, AND START YOUR PATH TO FINANCIAL FREEDOM

KAREN AGUAYO BATES, CPA

LEGAL AND COPYRIGHT

Copyright ©2017

ISBN: 9781549830723

Independently published

Published By:

Karen Aguayo Bates, CPA
San Diego, CA 92108
Karen@Mil-Loans.com
www.Mil-Loans.com

(619) 422-5900

First Edition

ALL RIGHTS RESERVED. No part of this publication may be reproduced, distributed, or transmitted in any form or by any means, including photocopying, recording, or other electronic or mechanical methods, without the prior written permission of the publisher, except in the case of brief quotations embodied in critical reviews and certain other noncommercial uses permitted by copyright law.

DEDICATION

To my best friend, business partner, and husband.
Thank you for your encouragement, love, and advice.
Thank you for the time and space to write this book!

To my Elizabeth for sharing her mommy with the world!
I know you love it best when we are together and cuddling!
I love you sweetheart!

I am so grateful for the opportunity of our great nation, the United States of America. Thank you for taking this young, first generation American from Los Angeles, giving her a place to grow up (the Navy), and allowing for some amazing benefits afterwards like the VA Home Loan!

The Home Buying Journey

Part One: Make the Decision to Buy

Chapter One. A Missed Opportunity

Chapter Two. A Man is not a Financial Plan… but a Home is!

Chapter Three. Security when Starting Over

Part Two: Crossing the Finish Line

Chapter Four. Have a Big Why – And Remember It!

Chapter Five. Get a 2nd Opinion

Chapter Six. Go the Distance!

Part Three: You Said Yes! What's Next?

Chapter Seven. Have a Long-term Mindset

Chapter Eight. When it's 'Not Now'!

Chapter Nine. VA Myths Debunked

A Final Message from Me to You

About The Author

Introduction

In this easy to follow, humorous, and quick to read book, my hope is to change the way you think about home ownership and more specifically, your unique home buying journey!

Why? Because the very act of moving is stressful enough. Add to that, the challenge of finding a safe neighborhood, a new mechanic, hairdresser, doctor, dentist, and schools for the kids.

Unfortunately, I found that our family could move as many as three times in just four years! This left us and many of our fellow Veterans living with what we refer to as, the rent trap. The trap of multiple moves causing enough stress that we avoid the added pressure of finding a home to buy. Besides, we would tell ourselves, homes are too expensive, real estate is unpredictable, and applying for a loan is scary and just adds one more big decision to my very long 'to do' list!

And yet, when my husband and I made the tough decision to buy a home and keep it for a while, we found we made lots of money! Not only for our own family, but then we heard story after story where Veterans everywhere and their families have been able to build up equity and create great financial options from the simple, but never easy act, of buying a home.

Now, let's get started on your journey!

Karen Aguayo Bates

PART ONE

MAKE THE DECISION TO BUY

From Ranks To Riches

Chapter One

A Missed Opportunity
My Six Figure Home Buying Mistake
I Chose Poorly!

Dear younger me,

You are going to hate this story but it needs to be told and I hope you listen. My wish is that it gets shared with everyone who enters the military, whether enlisted or an officer, in the hopes that it doesn't become their story.

And don't worry, it has a happy ending!

Heartbroken and wiser, Your future self!

When I sat down to sign my paperwork and get the keys to my new condo, I couldn't believe it. First I noticed that my payment was a couple of hundred dollars higher than what I was expecting. Then as that started to sink in, the nice sales lady sitting in front of me also shared that she needed another $2,000 from me as a down payment. Wait, what?

Why hadn't she called me?

It was 1994, there were no cell phones and I had just checked in at the base after a PCS move. I was staying in a rented room for two weeks with no telephone. In her defense, she hadn't been able to call me to give me the news because she didn't have a number for me.

As I stared at the papers, my mind started doing the math. The condo was already a stretch, my car was paid off but it was five years old and showing signs of wear and tear, and a few of my co-workers in the air traffic control tower had just reminded me that buying a home was a dumb idea because I was never going to be able to afford it.

I kept staring at the papers, taking some time for the realization to sink in that there was no way I wanted to take on that payment. As the reality sunk in, I could feel the pain physically. It was like hitting a wall. My stomach started turning, my head started to hurt, and I could feel the tears building.

Don't cry Karen, hold it together, do not cry! But it was too late.

As I tried to speak, the tears started flowing. I went from confident and excited to humiliated and shocked in a matter of minutes.

I explained that there was no way I could afford that payment. Over and over in my head, I heard the words from my unsupportive co-workers as I left the tower, "don't be stupid. You can't afford to buy a home. What are you thinking?"

Embarrassment and shame washed over me again. I'll never forget how I felt in that moment. I only wanted to get out of there and forget the entire experience.

And then another wave of panic hit me. I suddenly remembered the $1,000 I had given her three months earlier when I signed the contract to buy the place.

"Will I get my money back?" I asked her between sobs.

"I am so sorry Karen," she reassured me. "I will do everything I can to get your money back to you since the condo isn't VA approved. Because of that, I believe I can get your money back."

I did get my money back. And then I did something that made me feel a lot better. I rented a place, shifted my focus on learning the new airport for my work, and I bought a new car, a Camaro.

That was familiar. That is what everybody else was doing. That is what felt good.

That was also the worst financial decision I ever made.

Sadly, I wouldn't even realize it until almost 11 years later. The good news is, I did realize it and now I am sharing this with you.

Again, my dream is that you will understand how the decision I made was in hindsight, a mistake. And more importantly, you will have the wisdom to make great choices from hearing this story.

11 YEARS LATER
(YES, IT REALLY TOOK 11 YEARS TO GET THIS!)

Rick was screaming and swearing at me through the phone. Although I don't think you should yell and swear at people no matter how angry you are, I understood why he was angry and especially, why he was angry at me. And I felt terrible.

The condo he was trying to buy before he left on deployment was not going to close for 30 more days. It was getting delayed because it wasn't VA approved and I needed 30 more days to get it to the VA Regional Loan Center for approval. He didn't have 30 days. His ship was leaving and his wife needed a place to live.

His wife was a friend of mine so I offered to let her stay with me until I could fix it. I needed to fix it. He hung up on me. Later, she sent me a note saying we were no longer allowed to be friends. I never heard from her again.

It was my first VA loan as a loan officer in the mortgage industry. I knew condos needed to be approved and I had requested the VA number from the sales office. They sent me a number.

Unfortunately, it was for the builder of the condo and not for the actual condo complex, which also needed its own approval number. By the time I realized the error, it was going to delay the closing. And I shared how that ended when I gave the news to my friend.

The year this happened was 2005. Eleven years after my own condo nightmare. In that time, I had left the military, married Ken, and moved three times in four years.

I had learned that the very act of moving was stressful enough. Add to that, the challenge of finding a safe neighborhood, a new mechanic, hairdresser, doctor, dentist, and schools for the kids.

We didn't have kids. I'll share that part of our story in a moment. Most of my friends did have kids and I knew the school thing was a very big deal. I had been inspired to start a mortgage company. One of my goals was to protect my friends by giving them someone they could trust to do their mortgage loan when they moved. And to make the decision of buying a home less stressful!

At that moment, for Rick and his wife, I had a major fail. I still feel bad about letting them down. If you are reading this, I'm so sorry Patty. Luckily, I never let that happen again.

And then as I sat feeling terrible, I had an old painful memory pop up and I realized something I had not known before.

My own condo failure was avoidable.

It was completely foreseeable!

The sales office and the nice sales lady didn't know when I started the process, when they took my money, and when they gave me hope I would qualify that the condo needed to be approved.

Unfortunately for all of you reading this, it still happens today. I see it happening and I hate it.

They say we remember things that happen as a significant emotional event. I can still remember the address of my condo. It was a significant emotional event for me.

45285 Keyport Court, California, Maryland.

In fact, it's my memory that prompted my husband to ask me to implement a rule in our home during arguments. His request was that I not bring up anything up that I am still angry about that happened over six months ago. Especially in the middle of a heated argument. He said it's useless because he can't defend himself against any claims I make. He sincerely cannot remember those details. It's a good rule. I abide by it and it has helped our relationship tremendously!

I did remember the condo though and I do bring it up. I even looked it up online. I still do that today sometimes to see how much it's worth.

That condo that I didn't buy is now worth about $200,000. My mortgage loan, after 23 years, would be less than $50,000. In other words, today, I would have made over $100,000 if I had purchased that condo and kept it.

I know there are other things to consider. But NAS Patuxent River is a base that has grown quite a bit. And if you look up the address, the condo is literally 5 minutes from the gate. Also, there were other condo's in the area that were VA approved.

Had I understood money and understood why I needed to stick to my decision to buy a home, I could have easily walked down the street and bought a different condo. One with an affordable payment that would not have required any money down.

I didn't have anyone telling me that the Camaro would be worth $150 in scrap metal and that my condo would be worth over $100,000. My daughter is 11. That would be a great start to her college fund, her wedding, or our retirement. I can think of a LOT of things I could do with that money.

I simply didn't know.

And here's the funny part, sitting down to write this to you has made me really think through the details. I want to get them right. I have always said over the years as I have told this story, that the agent and lender didn't know enough about the industry to help me get into a home when it was the perfect time for me to buy.

But sitting here this morning and mulling this over for the last few months, I honestly don't remember exactly how I ended up in that sales office at the condo. It was 23 years ago and I don't journal so I can't go back. What I do remember vividly are the numbers and how I felt.

What I often don't remember in my memories are the people. I have the same problem when I look at my high school yearbook. Can you relate? I have a task brain and a "to do list" brain. I have always been focused on tasks, never people and that is something I am currently working on in my life today.

My takeaway from this though, knowing the amazing REALTORS® I know today, how hard they work and how much they care about homeownership and their clients. I either wasn't working with the right agent or I simply found that office on my own. They are advocates and the good ones will do what they can to get you and your family into a great home!

The people you choose to work with in the process are the most critical decision to your success when buying a home.

I love what one of my coaches once said about who we choose to work with. He said, and I summarize, the success you will have in a relationship with any person professionally is based on two things; their personal life and their past performance. I won't argue with anyone on this point. What I can say is that the older I get and the more experiences I have, I find those words to be true in pretty much all life situations.

It has now been 23 years since my condo fiasco. What I want to emphasize is that we are all on a home buying journey.

The only difference between success and failure on that journey is whether you make wise decision to buy when you have the choice.

THE 3 DECISIONS TO CROSSING THE FINISH LINE ON YOUR HOME BUYING JOURNEY.

Here are the three major lessons I learned that I will be sharing with you throughout this book.

1. Make the decision to buy a home. Financially, it is a wonderful long-term decision for you.

2. Get a second opinion. Condo issues are only one of the many issues that you could potentially run into when using your VA loan.

3. Go the distance! Like marriage and having kids, there will be difficulties, doubts, delays and even dead ends. But in the end, they are all worth the effort!

Will you say yes to your home buying journey?

My goal is to get you to say yes to trying.

Not necessarily yes to home ownership because you won't really know what you want to do until you see the numbers.

But yes, to considering it, to calling a company like ours. In fact, I hope you call right now!

As we like to say at the office, the answer to the homeownership question should never be a no.

It should always be a yes or a not now. But never a no!

Will you say yes to trying? I sure hope you do!

Chapter Two

A MAN IS NOT A FINANCIAL PLAN...
BUT A HOME IS!

A HAPPY ENDING

Dear younger me,

Four years after you chose to buy a Camaro instead of a condo, you married Ken. Ken owned a home. That was wise!

Congratulations, Your Future Self!

I've always loved that meme with the old, bald, heavy set man with a beautiful young girl on his arm in a bikini. The caption reads:

Boys: this is why you should study hard in school.
Girls: this is why you should study hard in school.

Funny but wrong, I know. Also, sometimes true.

Ken is two years younger than I am and he was a mere 25 when he arrived in Virginia Beach and bought a home. All his squadron buddies were buying. I remember how excited I was when I saw our beautiful, two story home on a huge, corner lot.

I had moved to Virginia Beach but wasn't working full time because I wanted to go to college and get my degree. I had served my eight years in the navy and I was feeling a little behind on life milestones at my ten-year high school reunion that summer. Most of my high school friends were married, with college degrees, and some with kids even.

Why do we do that to ourselves? Compare ourselves to others instead of focusing on the benefits of our circumstances. In hindsight, I guess it was because I didn't see the benefits.

Yet, going to college after the navy was a great opportunity. I ended up as valedictorian and gave the commencement speech at graduation. I was not the smartest person in my class. But I can say I was very serious, intense and focused about my studies. I worked harder on my courses than I would have straight out of high school. And so, I ended up in college full time the first three years of our marriage.

Most of Ken's squadron buddies were what we referred to as "dink's", dual income, no kids. We were living on one income. I soon realized we were also living across town from everyone else. And then I felt embarrassed, maybe even jealous.

I believe this happens today. Where we want to live and where we can afford to buy a home are mutually exclusive.

I know this feels terrible. Luckily, I didn't have any influence over Ken when he bought the home. It was perfect for us and when we moved, we rented out the home. Just seven years after Ken bought the house, we sold it and made just over $65,000.

The even better news is that I survived the three years we lived in the home very easily and it was a great rental property. In the end, Ken had us living within our means and I am grateful for that. It is a rare quality and one I have grown to appreciate. Also, a habit I have grown to not only admire but develop in myself – staying in budget. A wise person once told me that we never have a money problem, we have a management of our money problem which is so true!

The good news from that decision doesn't end there.

We used the $65,000 as a down payment to purchase a home in San Diego when we arrived in 2003. That home went way up in value. It did drop later when the market crashed but we had a payment we could afford, we kept the home, and over the last 14 years since we bought the house, it has increased quite a bit in value.

We still own it today and keep it as a rental property. I love this home. Not the house itself. But I love that this San Diego home gave me options the moment when I needed it most in my life! It was the moment that our fairy tale plan ended with one phone call!

MONEY GIVES THE GIFT OF OPTIONS

As I hung up the phone, I could hear his words, over and over in my head.

The doctor said my sperm count is zero. Not low, it's zero. It echoed in my head…Zero. Zero. Zero.

Now, I am not a fertility specialist by anyone's account but I did know one thing. A zero-sperm count was bad. And the doctors were right. Ken and I could not have a biological child.

As devastating as that news was, being a problem solver and a planner, I had a bigger problem that my brain wanted to tackle. My well laid out plans were going up in flames.

After three tax seasons, I had discovered that the degree I had worked so hard to get in accounting, followed by the CPA license I had strived to power through, and the masters of taxation I sacrificed for, all combined to land me into a career that I didn't exactly enjoy.

Even worse, I was good at it!

How is that worse? I was right on track in getting promotions and making good money. But deep inside, I died a little each day. Okay, maybe not that dramatic but in the long run, I may have literally died of boredom. We will never know.

Here was my plan, marry a great guy – check!

Get your degree so you will always have a back-up plan, the ability to get a good job, and a way to earn good money – check!

After 4 years and 3 months of marriage, get pregnant and have a baby because Ken wants to wait 5 years – check!

Except that in the month of our 5-year wedding anniversary, instead of having a baby, I had the call from Ken that changed our lives.

We knew we could adopt. We had always felt an urge to adopt. So, I was sad, but not exactly devastated. If you remember, my brain prioritizes tasks over circumstances. This means I tend to think through problems when I encounter them.

As a result, I was more worried about my current problem, how was I going to endure two more tax seasons as adoptions took a LONG time no matter how much research I did on our options? And even though it was May, I found myself dreading all the adorable Christmas cards of my wonderful friends and their perfectly cloned children, one boy and one girl. Perfection!! Or for me, ouch! The thought of it hurt.

I needed to make a change and quickly! I needed a challenge, a new plan.

The good news was that once again, Ken had set us up for success. It seemed like everyone lived in Poway, which was expensive, for those coveted school districts. Ken and I had once again landed on the "old side of town", living on one paycheck, and we were ready for me to stay at home with our 2.0 kids.

That obviously didn't happen.

What did happen though was our house had increased in value, a lot. And after doing my sister's tax return for three years, I realized I was in the wrong industry. She was in the mortgage industry and had quadrupled my taxation income. If I had to keep going to the office, I wanted to work in an industry where I had the potential to make great money. And finance, mortgages specifically, was that industry.

Adoption was expensive! $20,000 to $40,000 were the numbers we were given. I was a woman on a mission. Change the world and make great money so I could adopt my babies!

Two weeks after my call from Ken, I quit my taxation job and landed a sales job in the mortgage industry.

It only took seven months of working in the mortgage industry to become so disgusted by the attitude of "profits over people", that I quit. I quit and took out a home equity line on our home. Then I wrote a business plan to start Military Home Programs, Inc. (now Military Home Loans).

I had options.

Living within our means, living on the other side of town from our friends, and buying a home gave me options.

We still run that business today as Military Home Loans. We do VA loans across California and help veterans find great lenders across America.

The first five years were crazy and taught me what not to do as a woman in business. They are the same rules we should apply to home ownership. Don't follow the crowd and do what everyone else is doing. Know what you want to achieve and go for it.

And seven years ago, I even bought my dream home!

At the age of 40! Finally!

But here are the takeaways I want to share with you.

THE 3 BENEFITS FROM KEN'S WISE CHOICE OF BUYING A HOME

1. He purchased a home we could afford and always on one income. The lower price and mortgage, made it easier to find a renter when we moved. This allowed us to rent the home long enough for it to increase in value before we sold it.

2. When we sold his home, we reinvested the profit into another home purchase vs spending the money.

3. We took the money from our second home and invested it in starting a business. We had options!

From Ranks To Riches

CHAPTER THREE

SECURITY WHEN STARTING OVER

"It's said that a wise person learns from his mistakes. A wiser one learns from other's mistakes. But the wisest person of all learns from others' successes."

John C. Maxwell

When Gerri-Lynn joined the navy, one of the first things she did was buy a home. And like me, she was advised against it by many of her well-meaning friends and the influencers in her life.

Luckily, unlike me, she did it anyway. Go, Gerri-Lynn!

And I am so glad she did. Because a decade later, Gerri-Lynn was married, had two young boys, and she was getting divorced.

Sadly, we see this a lot in our precious military family.

During the divorce, her home, the one she bought before she was married, stayed out of the divorce settlement.

After the divorce, Gerri-Lynn sold her home, took the cash, and started a new life for her and her two sons.

Today, she too is in the real estate industry. I know her because she has the same passion I do for seeing our friends make the right decision when it comes to a home.

THE 3 TAKEAWAYS FROM GERRI-LYNN'S WISE DECISION TO BUY A HOME

1. She purchased it when she was single and had many years left in the military. We normally are not thinking of buying a home at this point in our lives. Gerri-Lynn did and I hope you do too!

2. She bought smart with a long-term, fixed payment. She kept the home and rented out the property for years while she served her time in the military. And she allowed the time needed for her home to increase in value.

3. After her divorce, she sold the home and restarted her life with her two young sons. She had more financial security and peace than many of our friends do during their divorces.

Wouldn't it be great to have this kind of peace of mind in the midst of a tragedy?

THANK YOU GERRI-LYNN FOR SHARING YOUR STORY AND ENCOURAGING US TO MAKE BETTER DECISIONS AND LIVE WITH FEWER REGRETS!

A TALE OF TWO VETERANS

I enjoy reading the Wall Street Journal. And one of the greatest impacts they have had over the years in story telling or story selling as I like to call it, is their concept of, "a tale of two." It's the one where two guys grow up together in the same town, they go to the same college, get married, have kids, and they even work in the same company.

Here is where the story separates. One is the CEO and the other is not. The difference? You may have guessed it, the CEO read the Wall Street Journal.

Isn't that a great story? The tale of two is a powerful way to help our brains understand how decisions impact us in the long run.

So here is my tale of two veterans to help us remember and easily share the difference buying a home can make in the long run. It is a true tale but one where I have changed the names.

THE SMALL DIFFERENCE THAT HAD A BIG IMPACT:

MEET MIKE AND BOB

Mike called me because he knew we had started a mortgage company and he had two condominiums he wanted to refinance. He was retiring from the military after 33 years and he wanted the cash to build his dream home.

Get this, he had purchased two condominiums at his first couple of duty stations about 30 years earlier.

They were both almost fully paid off and they were worth about one million dollars at the time he called me!

He had always rented them out so someone else had paid the mortgage payment all those years.

Contrast that with Bob's story. He was retiring after 32 years in the marine corps. Yet, he and his wife had never bought a house. And I understood completely why they had not.

They had four kids and they moved often. Renting or base housing had always been the choice they felt comfortable with making. I watch my friends make this same choice every day. Yet, when Bob was leaving the military, he had no savings and he didn't own a home.

It's still hard to believe. The only difference in the two situations was the choice to buy a home. And it literally made a million-dollar difference in the long run.

This is a good time to mention why we don't buy.

The very thought that we would need to spend money fixing up the place and keep an emergency fund on hand is daunting. What if someone moved out unexpectedly and stopped paying their rent?

These thoughts and uncertainties can leave us feeling scared or overwhelmed. I know because I personally overestimated the current pain of the costs and didn't understand I would be better off focusing on the long-term benefits of owning a home.

When I wasn't aware of the benefits, I only had fear of the unknown as my focus. I could always find a million reasons why it wasn't the right time or worth the time and energy to do the harder thing.

Luckily, right now you can look at someone else's success and have 20/20 vision on the past based on their story. Then, it is just a matter of making it your own!

Again, there is no crystal ball in this world but if you look at all the very rich folks in America, they are usually business, land, and home owners!

Loaded with all this information, my one question to you is this; will you make the decision to give it a try? This is not a commitment to buy. This is a commitment to getting to your own yes or not now answer.

If the answer is yes, then keep reading as I want to ensure you have the 3 key decisions you must embrace to cross the finish line!

Dear Younger You,

Congratulations on making a wise decision!

Your future self.

THE 3 TAKEAWAYS FROM A TALE OF TWO VETERANS

1. Purchasing a home is a bigger commitment and takes more time, energy, and planning than renting a home.

2. Purchasing a home can make a very large difference in your financial position when you retire.

3. Purchasing a home is worth considering as early as possible. Having a home you can sell when you leave the military will help you to save money simply by holding onto the property as you pay down the mortgage.

It's not magic, it is just math!

From Ranks To Riches

PART TWO

YOUR HOME BUYING JOURNEY:
3 KEY DECISIONS TO CROSSING THE FINISH LINE

From Ranks To Riches

CHAPTER FOUR

HAVE A BIG WHY – AND REMEMBER IT!

"The most critical factor subduing the demand for housing is that home ownership is no longer seen as the great, long-term buildup in equity value it once was."

- Mortimer Zuckerman

I have no idea who Mortimer Zuckerman is but he has a point. He's not saying that home ownership is no longer a great, long-term builder of equity value. He is saying it is *no longer seen as the great, long-term buildup in equity it once was.* In running a business, I have seen first-hand that perception is reality. And the dream of buying a home is not nearly as glamorous as in the past.

How do you see home ownership? Do you believe it allows a great, long-term buildup of equity?

The long-term buildup of equity is in my opinion, the best benefit of owning a home. But, considering the quote, I am going to focus on three other benefits I enjoy in addition to the equity buildup!

My goal is that this chapter will help you believe buying a home is a great investment once again! Here are three reasons I personally believe in home ownership.

3 WAYS BUYING A HOME SAVES YOU MONEY – EVEN IF THE MARKET STAYS FLAT!

#1 - BUYING A HOME MEANS YOUR MONTHLY HOUSE PAYMENT STAYS THE SAME

In the financial industry, we have a fancy phrase for a long-term fixed payment that does not increase when everything else you purchase in life does. Think gas, food, and clothing. It's called a *hedge against inflation*.

Unlike your option of renting, buying a home and getting a mortgage offers you peace of mind with a consistent, fixed payment over the life of the loan. This benefit of a mortgage will save you money.

While renting, each year as your lease expires, your landlord may take this as an opportunity to raise your rent when you renew your lease. You may have already experienced this if you are renting now.

OUR SAN DIEGO HOME

On our investment home in California, the one we bought when we moved here in 2003, we have been renting out the home for seven years now. It's a standard, three bedrooms and two bath home, close to everything. The annual inflation and demand over the last 7 years has allowed for a $50 increase each year in rent.

Over the past six times we have renewed the lease, we didn't make the increase. Then this past summer, we hired a new property manager and the next thing I knew, she informed me that she was renting the home for $300 per month more than we started at seven years ago when we moved out of the home. It's still hard for me to believe that rents have increased that much in our city.

If our original tenants had purchased the home, the payment may have started a little higher initially, but imagine the money they would save over a 30-year period by buying versus renting the home! The savings potential adds up quickly!

If you are renting now, how much has that rent increased in the past year or two for you?

I know buying can be scary and housing prices are high. But if you can find a home you can afford to buy today, isn't it nice to think about how much money you will be saving over the next several decades as rental prices increase all around you?

Before we move on to the second way buying a home saves you money. I want to quickly mention why you sometimes hear that a mortgage is increasing. Why? Because I am saying it doesn't increase so I want to give you the full picture in case you see or hear that it does increase. This will lead to confusion and when we are confused, we don't buy.

Two Reasons a Mortgage Payment Might Increase

The first reason is that someone may have taken a loan that is only fixed for a short period of time. With mortgages, you have options to choose from. Think of car loan options.

You can take a lower payment over more years of paying the loan back. I've seen seven years or more. Or you can take a higher payment and pay off the loan in less years.

For a mortgage, you have options too when it comes to how many years you want to pay back your loan and these can range from 15, 20 and 30 years (or longer in some cases). The other option is deciding if you want the loan to have a fixed payment the entire life of the loan. I sincerely don't want to lay out the options here as they change like the weather in some areas. I do want you to know that you have choices.

Now for the second reason.

The Foursome: Principal, Interest, Taxes and Insurance

For a fixed payment on your mortgage loan, let's use your car loan for comparison. Like your car loan, the actual loan portion of the mortgage payment, the principal and interest, is fixed.

And like your car, your house requires two other payments, property taxes and insurance. For your car, this is usually your annual motor vehicle registration and your auto insurance that increase each year.

This is no different than your home loan except that with your car, the four items are not paid together. This makes it less confusing and more obvious what is increasing each year. The car loan itself, does not.

With a home mortgage, these four items, principle, interest, taxes, and insurance can be lumped together in one big payment so it may not be clear to you what is increasing each year. If you use your VA loan benefit, these four items will automatically be lumped together for one large payment. I still want you to have peace of mind that the loan portion, if you have a 30-year fixed, is not the portion that is increasing. I don't have a crystal ball but my prediction is that property taxes and insurance will continue to increase each year. Do you agree?

The Finish Line

Eventually, if you make your payments every month, the car is yours! Unfortunately, even when you reach the finish line, you do still have to register the car each year, pay for auto insurance, and hopefully you take it in for maintenance to keep it running smoothly and safely, but the loan is paid off.

Your home mortgage works the same way! You may need to replace a water heater, your insurance will need to be paid, and your property taxes may increase too. But your loan will go to zero and eventually, you will own your home! It's that simple.

A Reason to Believe in Home Ownership

Your payment will stay the same regardless what the economy is doing. I once heard at an investors meeting that we are the only country in the world that allows a fixed interest rate and payment on real estate. The speaker stated this fact as the reason we have many foreign investors buying land in America. Isn't that interesting?

I haven't visited all other countries nor fact checked his statement. I do wonder if it is true for all foreign lands. Either way, I know it is an opportunity for us and I do feel sad when I read Mortimer's quote.

And I even know who he is now! The CEO of Boston Properties, the editor in chief of US News and World Reports, and an 80-year-old man with a nine-year-old child. That is impressive! Thank you, Wikipedia!

#2 - Buying a Home is a Forced Savings Plan

I'm sitting here trying to figure out how to make this section more entertaining. I'm failing.

Maybe I should just state the facts and wrap the chapter up?

Or, maybe you should grab a cup of coffee and I'll keep this short! It's important. I promise!

Remember when I shared that every month when you make your loan payment, you pay principal and interest? Principal is the part of the loan that decreases the loan balance each month. Interest is the portion you pay for the benefit of borrowing the money in the first place.

The most common loan we work with is a 30-year fixed loan. With a 30-year fixed loan, you make your payment for 30 years and your loan is paid off.

If you've ever paid off a car loan, you know the feeling of not having a payment. It's exhilarating! I haven't paid off a home yet but I like knowing that in 16 years, my first San Diego house will be paid off and I will be 64 years old.

At that point, I can continue to rent the house and collect a nice income or I can make the decision sell the home. Our neighbor just sold a similar floor plan for $100,000 more than we bought our house for in 2003. That gives me hope that whether we rent out our home in the future or sell it, it will have been a great savings plan because of the principal we paid each month.

Think about the benefit of how this works. Some may argue it is not a savings account but to me, it has the same outcome. If I put that same amount of money towards rent, there would be no long-term benefit. When we pay a home loan because we purchased a home, we get the home.

A Forced Savings Plan

There is both good news and bad news when you think about principal. The good news is that you are paying down a loan and will own your home. The bad news is that if you were saving that same amount in a savings account, you could easily access the money you put into the account.

This is the reason I call it a "forced" savings plan. You are forced to save the money and you don't have the option to remove it quickly and easily. But forced is not always a bad thing if you have trouble saving money and leaving it in the bank versus buying a new car.

If you read my bio, you will see my friends call me the Queen of Reframe. In this case, I believe the negative benefit of not being able to access your principal easily is a good thing because it forces you to save.

Remember when I shared that we sold Ken's first home in Virginia Beach when we arrived in San Diego? Between the principal we had paid down, and the increase in the market value over the six years we rented the home, we made over $65,000. And that was on a home that originally cost $116,900.

#3 - BUYING A HOME MAY SAVE YOU MONEY ON YOUR INCOME TAXES

Yes, I used the phrase "may save you money" on purpose. Each month you pay your home loan payment, you pay both principal and interest. We covered the benefits of paying off principal as a forced savings plan. The other benefit comes from paying the interest charged for having a loan.

If the total mortgage interest you pay for the tax year, along with other income tax deductions that are allowed, are higher than your standard deduction, you will save money on your income taxes. Depending on your tax bracket, this can create a nice break to your income taxes due.

One of my favorite parts of working as a mortgage loan originator was doing income tax projections for our clients. One, it allowed me to use my degree that I worked so hard to earn. That felt good. But more importantly, it gave our clients even more reassurance that buying a home would benefit them today and in the future. The first two benefits I mentioned are long-term. But the income tax savings is a benefit that you can enjoy from the start.

WHERE ARE THE NUMBERS AND FANCY FINANCE TERMS?

As a Certified Public Accountant (CPA), I could use a lot of fancy terms here to explain this section from a financial perspective. But fancy terms confused me a lot in school and I had to look up many of the words, more than once. I often read the dictionary's meaning of a word and thought, well why didn't they just say that?

Don't get me wrong, I do love numbers and I could give you spreadsheets showing you in extreme detail the data that backs up the statements I am sharing here.

In fact, one of my favorite sayings is, "it's not magic, it's just math." And I base many decisions on basic math.

But ultimately, I decided there are many books and investment guides that focus on that information. They explain in detail the math, the financial concepts, and the market data over the past decades. My goal here is share the information in a way that you can relate to. From veteran to veteran, and from my own experience verses that of a financial expert.

I believe in homeownership because of my financial education and expertise. But I believe in it even more because of my personal experience and the experience of many of my clients, friends, and family! If you want spreadsheets and data, please email me and we can geek out together over the possibilities and opportunities.

Until then, my hope is that you will make the decision to buy and create your own stories and numbers for proof to share with those around you!

A RECAP FOR WHEN THINGS GET TOUGH IN THE HOME BUYING PROCESS:

3 WAYS BUYING A HOME SAVES YOU MONEY – EVEN IF THE MARKET STAYS FLAT!

#1 - Buying a Home Means Your Monthly House Payment Stays the Same

#2 - Buying a Home is a Forced Savings Plan

#3 - Buying a Home May Save You Money on Your Income Taxes

Take a few minutes to write down what you remember from this chapter on the three benefits above. Then expand on the one that means the most to you and why.

You will want to reference this section and reinforce your "why" as you make your way through your own home buying journey!

From Ranks To Riches

CHAPTER FIVE

GET A 2ND OPINION

"If the world thinks you're not good enough, it's a lie, you know. Get a second opinion."

Nick Vujicic

I was amused by a cartoon I saw the other day. It showed a picture of a man on an exam table with a doctor standing in front of him with a clip board in hand and stethoscope around his neck. The caption, "I already diagnosed myself on the Internet. I'm only here for a second opinion."

DON'T TAKE "NO" FOR AN ANSWER

When Ken and I decided to buy a bigger home in San Diego, we decided to try out our favorite, local credit union. Even though we are lenders ourselves, it is a bit of a conflict of interest if we attempted to do our own loan. And, we wanted to experience the process for ourselves.

First, we applied and the next thing I noticed was that a portion of my checking account was frozen for the application fee and for the appraisal fee. Although that didn't make me happy, I didn't stop the process.

We submitted the paperwork and then waited for the answer. **And to my surprise, we were not approved!**

The requirement we did not meet was that they did not want to count the tenant's rental income for the home we were leaving behind. They wanted us to qualify for both mortgages at the same time!

Luckily, Ken and I knew to go to a different lender that would allow us to apply our tenant's rent toward the payment. We knew that this was the credit unions guideline, not the VA's. And since it was their money to lend, they got the final vote.

If you are scratching your head and asking how the VA loan is different at two different banks, I understand.

It's confusing. And it's true. And, it's the reason we all need to know to get a second opinion!

UNINTENTIONAL CONSEQUENCES

Did you know that the VA (Veteran's Administration) is not the one that lends you the money to use your VA home loan benefit?

They are not. They merely put basic guidelines together to oversee the benefit and they let the banks, credit unions, and other lenders lend the money.

The guidelines come to us in a document known as "The VA Lender's Handbook". The VA Lender's Handbook states, "A poor credit history alone is a basis for disapproving a loan. If the credit history is marginal, look to other indicators."

Herein lies the problem. The handbook does not go on to define the difference between a poor credit history and a marginal credit history. It also does not provide a minimum credit score! Isn't that interesting?

Normally, this is the first question you are asked when you apply for a loan. What is your credit score or how is your credit?

To me, it is interesting and it makes sense. If the VA created their own minimums, they could be limiting veterans benefits by limiting someone from lending them money. The goal of the entire VA Loan Guarantee is to ensure you get into a home when it makes sense.

This leaves their guidelines vague and leaves the lenders looking internally to set guidelines that help them stay fair in their lending to everyone.

WHAT ARE LENDER OVERLAYS?

Banks and credit unions have a responsibility to treat everyone equally when they apply for a loan. It's a law and a good one.

To ensure they banks treat everyone equally, banks often provide an actual minimum credit score and other rules in addition to the guidelines of the VA guide. These are known in our industry as "lender overlays".

Think of it this way. If you and I go into a credit union and apply for a loan, the credit union must treat us equally and fairly. And this is great. We all want the world to be fair! Unfairness is a big part of the problems we see in the world today.

For the credit union, it's a lot easier to say you are approved and I am not if they have a minimum credit score that is set for their company.

For example, the credit union has said the minimum credit score is 620 (and this is just an example). You are at 620 and I am at 619.

We are close but only you qualify for their loan.

It's fair. It's a number. It's something we can all agree upon. It makes it easy to prove we received equal treatment.

Even better for homebuyers, if you are a nationwide company who lends money, it can be the standard used for each one of us who applies for a loan. It doesn't matter where we live or who we speak to at their company.

You may be thinking, all of this sounds great, how is this a problem?

The problem is that every company that lends out money on VA loans gets to decide how they will define "poor" and "marginal" credit scores along with all the other items that are vague in the 16 Chapters of the handbook!

I GOT THREE DIFFERENT ANSWERS, I'M CONFUSED!

The important thing to remember is that when you and your REALTOR® ask three different lenders their minimum credit score for a VA loan, you may get up to three different answers!

Isn't that fascinating? It's also confusing. And when we are confused, we don't buy!

I always believed a loan was a loan and that the VA loan was the same everywhere. It is not. Look at my own personal experience. It is heartbreaking to me that the most influential credit unions that have won the trust of Veterans have some of the most restrictive guidelines. That was the case for myself. Luckily, we knew it was allowed so we only had to find a fellow lender that allowed the rental income to count and then, we bought our home!

One of my goals when we started our company was to be a VA Loan Resource Center for Veterans! We only do loans in California but we have friends in the industry across the nation. I have heard many horror stories from bad information being passed to Veterans. Many missed opportunities, offers to buy homes not being accepted, and many other issues.

Even worse, I frequently meet other lenders who insist to me that their bank doesn't have one single lender overlay. My favorite question is, "what's your credit score?" They proudly share with me their banks minimum score for VA loans. And then I spend the next few minutes explaining to them what they need to know. Sometimes, they don't believe me!

Why does this happen? If you have only ever worked at one bank, you may not realize that the guidelines they give you to learn and follow is their internal guidelines for VA with the overlays included.

They sincerely have no idea that they should read the VA Lender's Handbook and then ensure they find peers in the industry they can refer business to if their bank is restricted on the guidelines.

At the end of the day, the best advice I can share with you, it's advice I used myself when we were declined for a VA loan in 2010.

Get a Second Opinion!

3 REASONS YOU MAY NEED A 2ND OPINION:

1. The VA itself does not lend money to Veterans

2. You will encounter lender overlays. Banks, credit unions and other companies lend the money. They must be fair to their customers so they put in uniform standards (lender overlays) that are different for every bank!

The banks loan officer may not know about the VA Lender's Handbook and believe their guidelines are from the VA itself and what everyone uses.

You only have to ask a question about credit score to learn that you may get three different answers to the same question from three different lenders.

This causes confusion in the marketplace.

When we are confused, we don't buy.

3. Your VA loan approval can vary with *every* credit union and bank!

A denial or "no" from one bank or credit union does not mean you do not qualify to buy a home.

Some credit unions and banks can be more restrictive:

- ✓ when choosing credit scores,
- ✓ how they look at your income,
- ✓ how much money you need to have saved,
- ✓ whether they will count rental income, and
- ✓ how they look at your prior bankruptcy, short sale or foreclosure!

Get a Second Opinion!

Chapter Six

Go the Distance!

"I hated every minute of training, but I said, Don't Quit. Suffer now and live the rest of your life as a Champion."

~ Muhammad Ali

THE 4 D'S IN YOUR HOME BUYING JOURNEY

I shared with you how we had to get a second opinion in order to buy our dream home in San Diego. What I didn't mention earlier was that it was the third house we put an offer on!

What a nightmare that was!

We started shopping in 2008. The market was changing and many of the homes were owned by the bank which meant contracts could take months to get approved. Our first offer fell right into this timeframe. And even worse, at the end of the long waiting period, in our case, almost eight months, the offer was declined at the last minute because of an appraisal issue.

We were heartbroken. But we had a big "why" and we tried again.

By now, it was 2009 before we found another unique home we liked. We made an offer. And then, once again, we found ourselves with a broken contract after more than six months of working with the bank and the seller.

Doubts started creeping into my thoughts. This is too much trouble. It's not going to happen.

I love the shows Fear Factor and Wipe Out. They describe perfectly what I was feeling at the time.

And then I looked at the numbers, remembered our goals, and I knew we needed to keep working towards our dream of a home we could share with others in need.

I am so glad we did! But it wasn't easy!

Luckily, I have some great mentors in my life and here is what they taught me that kept me motivated to keep trying.

THE 4 STAGES TO YOUR DESTINATION!

Reaching every goal in your life means you will go through stages. John Maxwell calls it the Law of Process.

One of my favorite sayings is, "all frustration is a violation of expectations." I thought it would be helpful to share with you the stages we often see when we help our clients buy homes.

THE DREAM

Whether it's home ownership, landing a job you love, meeting the man or woman of your dreams, or starting a family, having a dream or desire is the beginning of reaching any goal.

Dreaming is fun and it's free. It doesn't cost you anything to dream until you make the decision to move forward.

THE DECISION

Initially, I thought making the decision was the difficult part. It was difficult to decide on a major in college, to decide what type of wedding to have, and to decide when to have children. The longer I live, the more I realize, the decision is not nearly as daunting as the next stage.

For me, it's because my dreams and my "why's" are big. I bet yours are too.

The decisions often seem like the natural next step in my life. For my husband, it's the opposite. He spends a lot of time looking at the potential downfalls of making a decision before deciding anything. In fact, we dated for four years before we got married.

No matter which way you approach it, once you decide to move forward, stage three will happen!

THE DIFFICULTIES; DOUBT, DELAYS, DEAD ENDS

I shared with you our home buying delays and dead ends. Looking back, I found it in other areas of my life too.

When Ken and I decided to have children, I mentioned we had to adopt. What I didn't say was that we spent the next 8 years of our lives in one form of adoption or another. And today, we have one living child!

We had difficulty, doubt, delays and dead ends, over and over, and over again through our six adoption attempts!

THE DESTINATION

And yet, when I hold my daughter tight in my arms, cuddling during movies, and eating sunflower seeds until our tongues hurt, I would do it all over again in a heartbeat!

Being a mom is one of the most difficult, challenging, and yet rewarding decisions I have ever dreamed of and done. Even though we hit dead ends that were crushing blows during our journey, it was worth every tear.

And the last home we bought. It has a turret just like you see in a castle. One of my favorite mommy moments so far was showing my daughter the castle theme we had painted in her room when she was four years old.

It took over two years to find and close on the home. But when we did, she was just old enough to be incredibly excited for her new room and the castle theme.

She loves it!

Two dreams enjoyed in one moment!

THE 4 STAGES TO YOUR DESTINATION!

1. Dream – We had a dream. In this case, it was to buy our dream home.

2. Decision – We made the decision to go for it. We made a choice to start shopping and choose a home to buy.

3. Difficulty – The difficulty can come in many forms; doubt, delays, and even dead-ends. In our case, we hit delays and two dead-ends.

4. Destination – Eventually, you reach the finish line. Now, it may not be the ending you want every time.

But usually, if you don't give up and if you remember your why, you will make it there!

Dear future me,

I am deciding in advance to not give up when things get tough! I promise!

You Got This!

Your Younger and Wiser Self

From Ranks To Riches

PART THREE
YOU SAID YES! WHAT'S NEXT?

From Ranks To Riches

Chapter Seven

HAVE A LONG-TERM MINDSET

"Successful homeownership is not just putting people into homes, it's also making sure people keep their homes."

Michelle Collins

Part of the reason we didn't buy, especially when we were active duty is because we were thinking short-term. When we arrived in Point Mugu, California, Ken had two year orders and we decided without thinking about it too much, that it didn't make sense to buy a house when you only had two years to own the home. Sound familiar?

As I look back, I believe this was another missed opportunity.

What if we had considered keeping the home when we moved and having a rental property in an area where there are two bases, Point Mugu and Port Hueneme, very close together?

3 TIPS ON A SOLID, LONG-TERM MINDSET

In light of this realization, here are three tips on how to create a solid long-term mindset when you want to buy a home but have orders that only have you at your new location for a year or two.

This will also bring you peace of mind in case you unexpectedly get orders in the middle of a tour you thought had you in one location for five plus years!

#1 BUY WITH A SAVVY INVESTOR'S PERSPECTIVE

Having a plan is everything. Consider the difference in buying with a plan to live in the home for two years and then rent it out for the next 28 years.

When you buy with the motive of renting the home later, you can consider upfront items like how much the property would rent for when you move. Make a note to ask your REALTOR® as you are shopping for homes, what it would cost to rent a home in the area along with the price of the home.

Is it enough to cover your mortgage payment? Will the difference between your rental income and the mortgage work for your budget and comfort level if the rental income is lower?

More importantly, would you be less picky?

Would you be willing to be less demanding when it came to layout, location, and size? Could you sacrifice some desires for two years, knowing what the property could mean for your financial future?

I think this was especially important when Ken and I didn't have a child. We would have been willing to put up with a lot of "not perfect" *if* we had been thinking long-term and looking at keeping a property as an investment versus the place we currently required to meet all our needs.

Once that window of opportunity passes, you don't get it back. Where are you at on your journey? Are you able to sacrifice?

Today, we have our family to consider. In our case, our daughter has Type 1 Diabetes and since her diagnosis, we made the decision to homeschool.

But what if you already have four kids, two jobs, and the need for a good school district requirement?

To you, I say, are you sure there are no options? There may not be, but it is worth asking. Are there any options that might seem crazy to those around you but you know it would work for you? Like living in the second or third best school district, homeschooling for a short period of time or trying a nearby charter school.

If you gave up what is typical and normal, is there an option to purchase a home that may not be in your dream area with the best school district? Here is why I don't believe so strongly in normal any longer.

When our daughter, Elizabeth, was first diagnosed with diabetes, two statements were made to us repeatedly. The first was, "we know you must be overwhelmed." I wasn't overwhelmed and every time I heard that statement, I felt frustrated.

I was whelmed. Wait, is whelmed a word? If not, why not? Anyway, I was not *over*whelmed. I was in "let's tackle this mode"!

The second statement we were told several times a day was, "*nothing* had to change and Elizabeth could still eat and do whatever she wanted."

Now, with this, I knew they were wrong. The day before she was diagnosed, she was not allowed to eat or do anything she wanted. Why would diabetes change that?

As far as nothing having to change, I believed that one! We would do this and nothing would change!

Twelve days after her diagnosis, I was driving Elizabeth to school when I realized I needed to stop and get gas. And then, with that realization, I started sobbing.

It wasn't about having to get gas. I dislike that task, but it doesn't make me sob. It was that we had been attempting to get back into our 'pre-diabetes' routine and everything was harder and took longer. I was beyond exhausted and frustrated.

Nothing was predictable. Not her blood sugar levels, her response to insulin, nor her response to different types of carbs. Breakfast alone was now a lab experiment that needed a warm up and a follow up to ensure we were in the proper blood sugar zone.

Because of the extra work, we chose to get up an hour earlier. But even with the extra hour in the morning, we had been tardy and even absent once, five of the previous six school days!

And that morning, the morning I started sobbing as I put my credit card in the machine to get gas, that was the morning we were finally going to make it on time. Until I realized, I needed gas.

Tardy again. Why was being normal so hard?

In that moment, I made the decision to change everything.

To this day, over three years later, we have never returned to a normal school situation and I love our schedule.

We use a charter school with a homeschool and day classes option. Elizabeth loves her teachers, we hire tutors to fill the gaps, and we are not in the best school district. She is thriving, meeting her grade level milestones, and we work from home when needed.

We are never scheduled to arrive anywhere before 9:30am when we used to be out of the house just after 7:00am! As a family, we make sleep and diabetes care a priority, we take time to make breakfast, we work out together, and then we get ready for our day! I sincerely wish I had considered other options before she was diagnosed.

Changing our schedule has changed our lives! Why don't we ever stop to think out of the box?

All to say, what options do you have? If you want to buy a home and cannot afford to buy in the best school district or nicest part of town, are there any other options for you and your family to consider?

Would you be willing to live in your second or third choice for neighborhoods if it meant buying a property you could use as an investment and possibly help you to pay for college later? Again, this isn't to put pressure on you. You may not have other options today.

But maybe, just maybe, you can consider other options with your next move! It's worth asking the question!

#2 WORK WITH A PRO

When Ken and I moved from Point Mugu to San Diego, he had three year orders so we decided to buy a home. At the time, Ken decided we didn't need a REALTOR® because he wanted to save money. We found soon after that the seller is normally the one who pays the REALTOR® commission for both the buyer and the seller.

It's a good deal for us as buyers! Find a REALTOR®.

Once we experienced enough hassle to even see the inside of homes for sale, we found a REALTOR®. I understand why this is important. Think of it from the seller's perspective. People have lots of personal items in their homes like medications, jewelry, and financial information. If you don't have someone who is professionally hired to represent and ensure the strangers coming into your home truly want to buy, it's a little frightening!

For us, a REALTOR® was necessary. It turns out, with Ken's personality, he really did need to see all the homes he could before he was sure we were buying the right one.

I decided to stay home while he went to San Diego for several weekends in a row and view as many homes as he could for his peace of mind. I asked him to narrow it down to his favorite five and then I would look at those homes.

It works for us. He found the final five. I looked at all five and found one of them to be my favorite of the five. That's the one we bought.

Marriage is a funny thing as married couples are generally incredibly opposite. Ken has a difficult time understanding how I can be so sure of my decision after only looking at five homes. I have a hard time understanding why he must look at all of them.

We know this about each other and we not only accept our differences but we embrace them. In fact, often, we count on them. If you are not married, you will still want to keep this in mind for the future. If you are married, you will understand why I am including this information.

How do you and your spouse differ? Do you also need to send your spouse out with a REALTOR® or are you the one who prefers to see all the neighborhoods? Either way, there is no right or wrong answer. And each of us has different needs so I hope you find a way to not only embrace them but to work out a plan to ensure you both feel comfortable with the purchase before you buy!

The other professional I recommend, in addition to a REALTOR® is a property manager when you rent out your home. I used to think it was better to do it ourselves and save money. In fact, we owned a copy of Renting Out Your Property for Dummies once.

Knowledge says it's math and you save when you do the work yourself. Wisdom tells me money is not the most important consideration. What about your time and peace of mind?

When we moved out of our first San Diego home, we believed the rent would be around two thousand dollars a month. I mentioned this to my friend who is a REALTOR® and luckily, she is also a property manager. She said she had forty tenants she worked with and she knew in our neighborhood, she could get twenty-two hundred for the rent.

That got me thinking. I had been set on the two thousand a month. If her fee was less than two hundred a month and she could rent our home for twenty-two hundred, I would be making more money than on my own.

We have been renting the property for seven years now. She has always had tenants in there, the net rental income is automatically deposited into my checking account, and we get a wonderful income tax form each year with the expenses and income laid out in a form that I hand to my tax preparer.

During the second year of renting, my neighbors called me concerned about the activity of some of the youths in our rental home. I simply passed the information on to my property manager. The call from my neighbor created some issues around liability and my responsibility to my neighbors. I was incredibly grateful to have a professional in place to navigate the process.

Ultimately, after several calls from neighbors, we chose to ask the tenants to move at the end of their lease. Again, all I did was let my property manager know the circumstances and ask her advice. The situation was awkward for me and I honestly have no experience in the laws and rules of renting out property. There is a lot to the process!

Once the tenants moved, my property manager called me and asked if she could replace the carpet, the garage door and some other small items. She had an estimate, a contractor ready to go, and the colors and supplies picked out for me.

One month later, the work had been done and new tenants were moving into the house. Can you tell I enjoy having a property manager?

At the end of the day, it does cost us eight percent of our rental income each month. For me, it is worth it.

My husband agrees although he manages our second investment property himself. Sadly, he doesn't give me a nice form at the end of the year with the income and expenses laid out. But for now, I know he enjoys saving money and he does a good job!

For that second investment home, we purchased that house directly from a seller we knew personally. The tenant was already in place when we assumed the VA loan on the property. If the tenant ever decides to move, we will hire a property manager because the home is out of state. Every situation is different.

Deciding your comfort level with renting a home on your own or paying for someone to take care of it for you is the most important decision. I sincerely wanted you to know what your options were and how that worked for us.

Ultimately, there is no right or wrong answer. It truly is a preference and your tolerance for what you feel comfortable handling. And now you have more information to consider when making the best decision for yourself.

#3 PREPARE FOR EXPENSES

My third and final tip for a long-term plan is and having money set aside for planned repairs, unexpected repairs, and any of the other surprises that come with life.

There are two steps to this. First, have an emergency fund.

In fact, even before you decide to buy a home, start saving money. I am often asked how much you need to have saved. A good rule of thumb is a minimum of three months of your monthly income. If you can, keep six months of your monthly income, even better.

Second, understand what it means to be financially healthy.

I have witnessed that budgeting money is most people's least favorite subject. I sincerely believe this is because no one has ever shown us how to understand our net worth. When you are focused on cutting back on expenses versus how much money you can save, it is demotivating.

Think of dieting. If you were only ever told to cut back on all the delicious food you love to eat, you would feel miserable. But when you step on a scale or look in a mirror, you get to choose whether or not you are in good shape. You can determine whether or not you are healthy.

Money is the same way. But the scale for money and financial health is not your income or your expenses, ultimately, it is your net worth. Why didn't anyone tell us this sooner?

Your net worth is what you are worth if you were to sell everything you owned and paid off all your debt. What would be left?

I used to use my income as the measuring tool because I wasn't even considering my net worth and financial health. I thought how much money I made determined how healthy I was financially. And then I became an accountant. I witnessed many people who had a great income, but they were not financially healthy. They simply had more debt and expenses than those of us who made less income. They spent everything they made and more. Even worse, no matter how much they loved or hated what they did to earn their high income, they were stuck because they had bills to pay. It happens so easily when you are not paying attention.

In this world, especially once you leave the military, your income will sometimes be higher and sometimes be lower than it is right now. You could lose your job, get sick, or your expenses could unexpectedly increase. I know ours did when Elizabeth was diagnosed with Type 1 Diabetes. All these uncertainties in life make it necessary for each of us to focus on how much money we can keep in the bank. Focus on your net worth!

Building your net worth and focusing on your financial health is simple but not easy. And, I know you can do it! It is simply creating a lifestyle where each month, you spend less than you make. This won't happen overnight. I will spend the next chapter sharing how we keep what I refer to as breathing room, in our budget.

Moving forward, I hope you always remember this. Your financial health is not determined by how much money you make. This should be a relief if you are an E-1 in the military which is where I started. Your financial health is determined by what you choose to do with the money you make. Will you focus on your net worth?

THE 3 TIPS ON YOUR SOLID, LONG-TERM MINDSET

1. Buy with a long-term plan in mind. This will help you recognize opportunities so that you don't miss them!

2. Work with a pro. Find someone who knows more about real estate buying and property management to guide you and ensure you don't make any foreseeable mistakes!

3. Prepare for expenses. Always keep an emergency fund in place for life's unexpected events. And focus on your net worth as your measuring tool for financial health, not your income.

Take a few minutes to write down what you remember from this chapter on the three tips above.

You will want to reference this section and reinforce your "how" as you make your way through your own home buying journey!

From Ranks To Riches

CHAPTER EIGHT

WHEN IT'S 'NOT NOW'!

"Real estate cannot be lost or stolen, nor can it be carried away. Purchased with common sense, paid for in full, and managed with reasonable care, it is about the safest investment in the world."

Franklin D. Roosevelt

If you have said yes to giving home ownership a try but you know you have some work to do on your financial health before you get started, here is the chapter for you.

This chapter is difficult for me to write. I am concerned about our country and so many families that I know are not financially healthy. It's troubling to me that many of us are about one paycheck away from homelessness and no one seems to notice how bad the situation is. It's staggering but true in my opinion. I hope this doesn't sound harsh. I want to help.

Here is the reality. For many families, credit cards are at their maximum limits, car payments are large and long-term, and savings is minimal, with most having no savings at all. Without a savings account, it would only take losing your income and a few months without a paycheck before you would be forced into some incredibly difficult decisions. Not to mention the stress this would put on your family, your relationships, and your health.

I heard it summed up this way; *As Americans, we keep buying things we don't need, with money we don't have, to impress people we don't like.* It makes me think of the picture I see at Christmas with the dog in a funny costume and the caption, "human, why you do this?" I love that meme.

Prior to marriage, Ken and I both had a habit of spending everything we made. It was never an income problem, it was simply a management of our money problem. When we got married, we somehow decided it was time to start saving. It seemed like the next grown up thing to do.

Married, check. Save for retirement, check!

In hindsight, we didn't have a system or a plan. We were lucky because we got used to living on one income while I went to college during the first three years of our marriage. That set us up for success and the ability to start a savings plan when I did start earning money. Now that I am approaching fifty years old, I am so grateful we created better habits together.

Today, we have a system and I am going to share it with you. If you decide to buy a home, and even if you don't buy, I hope you make the decision to create a system or plan to stay financially healthy.

3 HABITS FOR FINANCIAL HEALTH

#1 – KEEP GOOD RECORDS

If I were lost and called you for directions, what is the first question you would ask me? More than likely you would ask me, "where are you?"

To create financial health, you must know the same information. Where are you now? To do this, you have to keep track of where your money is going.

I think this may be the toughest one for most of us. But this doesn't have to be complicated. We use our credit card almost exclusively and then pay it off each month to keep track of expenses.

This method of tracking does not work if you don't pay your credit card off each month.

If you find you are not paying off your credit card, then use another method.

If you do use your credit card, make sure you pay in a timeframe that keeps you from having to pay interest. You will have all your expenses in one place and you might also enjoy the airline miles. We earn our miles with a Southwest card and it has saved us thousands of dollars in airfare.

Between the credit card statement and our bank statement, I can sit down and track where our money is going and more importantly, I can see exactly where we should cut back on our spending or how much a habit is costing us.

The method you use, whether an app, a transaction journal where you write everything down, or another system, is not as important as creating the habit and tracking your expenses consistently.

#2 – CREATE A PLAN

I once heard that you can tell someone's priorities by looking at their calendar and their checkbook. I believe this is true. How we spend our time and how we spend our money, reveals who we are and what's important to us.

First, my disclaimer. Ken and I believe in God so our financial plan is based on tithing first. I am not trying to offend you and if you don't have the same beliefs, please skip the tithing and put that money towards something else.

Ken and I work on a simple plan we call our 10/10/80 plan.

This represents the picture of our priorities. This means we are committed to giving the first 10% of our income in tithes, then we save or invest the next 10% of our income, and we live on the rest.

It's simple and it works.

Giving and saving 10% usually don't raise a lot of questions. Although, I would fill my emergency fund (three to six months of my monthly income) before I started saving a retirement fund. Other than that, it is just math.

But how do we manage the other 80%? Other than our mortgages, Ken and I have worked hard to stay debt free. And it is a great feeling to know that the only bill we owe each month is our current living expenses for food, personal expenses, utilities, and our mortgages on our home and our rental properties.

I wish everyone knew they could reach this goal. I wish everyone had this goal.

There are only a couple of ways to save money and pay off your debt. You can either make more money, reduce expenses, or pray for a large gift. They do sometimes come in the form of a re-enlistment bonus. But that is not a gift!

If you are up for a pay increase, start saving that money or pay off your debt. If you are not, then take a good look at your records and start reducing your expenses.

Remember my Camaro? That car came with a $336 per month car payment. When I started college after leaving the navy, I didn't want to work many hours so I decided to find a cheaper car. I sold my Camaro after three years of owning it. I didn't make any money and I didn't have to pay any money to sell it. I broke even.

I then bought a used Mazda. It got better gas mileage, it was in great shape, and it was only $4,000 which allowed me to pay it off with a $136 payment each month. It made college much easier for me.

I remember someone once asking me, didn't you sell your car because you couldn't afford it? I thought, no way! I sold my car because I didn't want to work the hours it would take to make the payment. Most of us can afford anything we are willing to work for. Is it worth it?

I didn't love the Camaro nearly as much as I wanted to enjoy my time at college. It was one of the best financial decisions I had made at that point in my life. I never regretted it!

#3 - FOLLOW THE PLAN

Your plan will not be perfect and as we all know, life happens. Ken and I follow the plan as well as we can. We don't compromise on our tithing, that one is a priority for us. But as our business grows, we are sometimes forced to invest in our business versus paying ourselves.

When this happens, instead of saving 10%, we dip into our emergency fund to carry us through financially until we start paying ourselves again.

I can think of three seasons where this has been the case over the last ten years. What we focus on during this season is getting back on track and overall, we have increased our net worth and stayed financially healthy during that time.

I just realized it is kind of like laying ourselves off, except we are still working. I may be the worst boss I've ever had!

That was a joke. I love being self-employed!

Please remember, there will be setbacks. But if you expect setbacks, recognize the gap as a setback, and don't give up, you will persevere. And overall, you will be creating a habit for a financially healthy lifestyle.

TAKEAWAYS FOR 3 HABITS OF FINANCIAL HEALTH

1. Keep good records. Every plan or system needs a starting point. Once you know where you are, you can make adjustments to get where you want to go.

What system will you use to track expenses?

2. Create a plan. A plan makes sure you are living your priorities. This feels great when you know you are giving it your energy and effort!

What simple plan would work for you?

3. Follow the plan. Life is full of surprises when it comes to our jobs and incomes, our expenses, and money. Financial health is not having a large nest egg or net worth. Financial health is committing to and implementing a plan where you are making more money than you spend. Follow the plan!

How will you remind yourself to expect and persevere through setbacks?

Take a few minutes to write down what you remember from this chapter on the three habits above.

You will want to reference this section and reinforce your "how" as you make your way through your own home buying journey!

From Ranks To Riches

CHAPTER NINE
VA MYTHS DEBUNKED

"If it's the truth that sets us free, isn't it true then that it is the lies that hold us captive?"

~Dr. Lance Wallnau

When I left the military, I had some well-meaning friends share with me that I lost my VA loan benefit because I didn't go pick up my certificate when I left the service.

I believed them. It wasn't until years later I knew that this was not true. This is not the only bad information on VA. There is simply nowhere to get the right information sometimes, especially when I didn't even know what questions to ask.

I wrote up this list of myths to make sure another veteran didn't miss the opportunity to buy a home because of bad information.

When we hear about our VA, we typically hear that our VA loan does not require money for a down payment, it has no PMI (private mortgage insurance like FHA loans), and that the interest rates are competitive. These are great benefits.

What I want to share here, in this final chapter, is the information I often don't see all over the internet.

Here are the top ten myths or misconceptions I hear from veterans about our VA loan benefit that may keep us from buying a home.

THE TOP 10 MYTHS FOR VA LOANS

MYTH #1 - MY VA LOAN ELIGIBILITY EXPIRES

Your VA loan eligibility does not expire. In fact, we have had a first-time homebuyer who was eighty-six years old purchase with his VA eligibility. He had served in the military over five decades earlier!

MYTH #2 – MY VA LOAN BENEFIT CAN ONLY BE USED ONCE

I once heard someone mention they were going to save their VA loan for when they got out of the military.

It is possible to reuse your VA eligibility. There are some limitations and rules. The important thing to remember is that you can reuse it. We personally have seen it used five times by one veteran.

MYTH #3 – MY VA LOAN IS ONLY FOR 1ST TIME HOMEBUYERS

The VA loan eligibility is not a first-time homebuyer program. The VA works great for your second, third, and dream home too.

MYTH #4 – I CAN ONLY HAVE ONE VA LOAN AT A TIME

You can have more than one VA loan at a time. It's not magic, it's just math! The term we use to describe how it works is partial eligibility. Basically, if you don't use your full eligibility on one property, you can apply that towards your next purchase. The best thing to do is know that it is possible and to ask when you go to purchase a second home with VA.

MYTH #5 – WHEN I USE MY VA, I DON'T HAVE TO HAVE ANY MONEY TO BUY A HOME

The VA loan is a great benefit because it allows us to buy a home without putting any money down on the purchase price. For example, if your home is $300,000, you can get a loan for $300,000. But this is not the whole story. Remember when I shared that buying a home was in many ways like buying a car? When we buy a car, there is the price we pay for the car and then all the additional fees, on top of the purchase price that we are required to pay.

With a car, you can usually get all the costs wrapped up into the loan. With a home, it doesn't work the same way.

The costs that go with the purchase of a home get complicated based on where you live and what type of home you are buying. The best advice I can give you is to find a lender you trust to walk you through the costs in the area where you are buying the home.

MYTH #6 – I DIDN'T GET APPROVED BY MY FAVORITE BANK SO I MUST RENT

Every lender has different guidelines, please get a second opinion and reference chapter five of this book.

MYTH #7 THE PROGRAM IS ONLY FOR VETERANS, NOT ACTIVE DUTY

Luckily for us, the program is for eligible active duty, retired, prior military, and reservists. You don't have to wait until you finish your service to use your VA.

MYTH #8 – BUYING A CONDO IS THE SAME AS BUYING A HOME

Remember my six-figure home buying mistake? It was because the condo complex had not been VA approved. If you find yourself wanting to buy a condo that is not VA approved, it takes some time and energy to get it done but you can get them approved.

MYTH #9 – QUALIFICATION STANDARDS ARE HARDER

Income and credit guidelines are generally easier. VA loans, in my opinion, make the most sense for many situations we run into as veterans.

MYTH #10 – I'VE DECLARED BANKRUPTCY OR I HAVE A VA FORECLOSURE, SO I CAN NEVER USE MY VA AGAIN

It is possible to reuse your remaining VA eligibility after a VA foreclosure. We can use your remaining eligibility. VA is also the most generous when it comes to a new loan after a bankruptcy. You generally only need two years.

I hope you found these myths helpful!

If you did, feel free to grab a copy of them from our Facebook page or email me for a copy to pass along to your friends.

It is difficult to compete with all the noise on the internet. It's one of the most frustrating aspects of business. Trying to break through the bombardment of advertisements and get a critical message with the right information out to the world.

I am so grateful you somehow found this book and that you are still reading!

A FINAL MESSAGE FROM ME TO YOU

As I was wrapping up this book, Ken and I were discussing all the information I shared on our homes and missed opportunities. We talked about why we sold, why we didn't buy, and most importantly, what different decisions would look like today.

We started adding up all our missed opportunities. He had lived in Pensacola in 1994 and then in San Diego in 1996.

What if he had purchased? We made a list and here is what it looked like:

A home in Florida.

A home in Virginia.

Two homes in Maryland.

And two more homes in California.

We had so many opportunities and we simply didn't recognize them.

We even looked up the first home he bought for $116,900 in Virginia Beach, Virginia. If you remember, we made $65,000 when we sold it in 2003. Today, that home is worth about $290,000 and our mortgage would only have nine years left. It looks like the rent in that neighborhood is at $1,700 and our mortgage was just under $1,000. Wow, we had never looked that one up before!

You would think this information would make us sad. But we laughed.

Yes, we could have made better decisions. But ultimately, we are thankful for what we have today. More importantly, it gives us the opportunity to share with you so that you can look at making your own wise choices for your future.

I don't know where you are in your military journey.

If you are just starting out, that is great! You have the information we all wish we would have had when we were in your shoes.

If you are at the end of your military journey, that's okay too. I meet a lot of people who are working to save up a down payment and wish they had a VA loan to use. You are still in good shape with your benefit.

The most important thing is that you make the decision to buy and you stick with it.

If you found this information helpful, I hope you will pass a copy of this book along to your friend. Or, they can watch my 15-minute book summary at:

http://bit.ly/FromRankstoRiches

Thank you for sharing this time with me.

I wish you peace, love and joy on your journey,

Karen

P.S. We've started this journey together. Please email me to let you know how you are doing! Would love to hear from you!

Karen@Mil-Loans.com

About The Author

KAREN AGUAYO BATES, CPA

Here is what I want to share with you...
Karen is known by all who love her as the 'Queen of Reframe' transforming every major (and minor) obstacle into an opportunity to excel! And after 48 years, there have been some crazy obstacles!!

Her ability to overcome and then excel, took her to National Stages. On stages, her authentic and open nature enables the audience to deeply connect with her, see themselves more clearly, and begin to believe in THEIR POTENTIAL!

In her words, 'I love it when others believe in their own potential and especially when they gain a fresh perspective. That newfound perspective, combined with confidence and courage, is what enables us to pursue our dreams and become unstoppable!!'

Here is the stuff I am supposed to share...
Karen was an Air Traffic Controller in the United States Navy serving for eight years. After the Navy, Karen earned her undergraduate degree in accounting graduating Summa Cum Laude, her Master's in Taxation, and her CPA license.
In 2004, Karen realized an opportunity to serve the military and founded Military Home Loans. Karen and her husband Ken have become the VA Mortgage Specialists in San Diego and have had the privilege of consistently closing a VA loan every 3 days.

Her passion is to ensure Veterans never miss the opportunity to experience their American dream.
Along with her passion for serving the military, Karen is an advocate for her industry and community and has served on boards and committees for the San Diego Veteran's Coalition, numerous REALTOR® organizations, she was the 2013 President for the San Diego Chapter of the California Association of Mortgage Professionals, and is the 2017-2018 State President for the California Association of Mortgage Professionals. Karen is California's 2013 Mortgage Professional of the Year and was featured on Yahoo Finance for earning and retaining $1 million as a female entrepreneur.

Karen is devoted to her husband of 19 years and is blessed with their beautiful daughter Elizabeth, age 11.

Find out more at www.Amazon.com/authour/KarenAguayoBates

Or visit www.Mil-Loans.com to learn more about your VA benefit and buying a home.

Made in the USA
San Bernardino, CA
25 April 2018